Alexander Pope

Letters of the late Alexander Pope, Esq. to a lady

Never before published

Alexander Pope

Letters of the late Alexander Pope, Esq. to a lady
Never before published

ISBN/EAN: 9783744741293

Printed in Europe, USA, Canada, Australia, Japan

Cover: Foto ©Lupo / pixelio.de

More available books at **www.hansebooks.com**

LETTERS

OF THE LATE

ALEXANDER POPE, Esq.

TO

A L A D Y.

Never before publifhed.

LONDON,

Printed for J. DODSLEY, in Pall-Mall.

MDCCLXIX.

ADVERTISEMENT.

THESE Letters, befides the *naiveté* of the ftyle, the quick fallies of an ingenious mind, and the graver obfervations of re-flection and judgment, difcover the Writer's Heart to have had a more amiable fenfibility, and to be tinctured with more good-nefs, than his other Writings of this fort do.

It may be proper juſt to mention, that the Originals of theſe Letters are in Mr. Dodſley's Poſſeſſion.

MR.

MR. POPE'S LETTERS.

LETTER I.

MADAM,

Twitenham, Oct. 18.

WE are indebted to Heaven for all things, and above all for our fenfe and genius (in what-

ever

ever degree we have it) ; but to fancy yourſelf indebted to any thing elſe,
moves my anger at your modeſty. The
regard I muſt bear you, ſeriouſly pro-
ceeds from myſelf alone; and I will
not ſuffer even one I like ſo much as
Mrs. H. to have a ſhare in cauſing it.
I challenge a kind of relation to you
on the *ſoul's* ſide, which I take to be
better than either on a father's or
mother's ; and if you can overlook an
ugly *body* (that ſtands much in the
way of any friendſhip, when it is between different ſexes) I ſhall hope to
find you a true and conſtant kinſwo-
man

man in Apollo. Not that I would
place all my pretenſions upon that
poetical foot, much leſs confine them
to it; I am far more deſirous to be
admitted as yours, on the more meri-
torious title of friendſhip. I have
ever believed this as a ſacred maxim,
that the moſt ingenious natures
were the moſt ſincere; and the moſt
knowing and ſenſible minds made the
beſt friends. Of all thoſe that I have
thought it the felicity of my life to
know, I have ever found the moſt
diſtinguiſhed in capacity, the moſt
diſtinguiſhed in morality: and thoſe

B   the

the moſt to be depended on, whom
one eſteemed ſo much as to deſire
they ſhould be ſo. I beg you to make
me no more compliments. I could
make you a great many, but I know
you neither need them, nor can like
them : be ſo good as to think I do not.
In one word, your writings are very
good, and very entertaining ; but not
ſo good, nor ſo entertaining, as your
life and converſation. One is but
the effect and emanation of the other.
It will always be a greater pleaſure to
me, to know you are well, than that
you write well, though every time

you

you tell me the one, I muſt know the
other. I am willing to ſpare your
modeſty; and therefore, as to your
writing, may perhaps never ſay more
(directly to yourſelf) than the few verſes I ſend here; which (as a proof of
my own modeſty too) l made ſo long
ago as the day you ſate for your picture,
and yet never till now durſt confeſs to
you.

Tho' ſprightly Sappho force our love and praiſe,
A ſofter wonder my pleas'd ſoul ſurveys,
The mild Erinna, bluſhing in her bays.
So while the ſun's broad beam yet ſtrikes the ſight,
All mild appears the moon's more ſober light,
Serene, in virgin majeſty, ſhe ſhines;
And, un-obſerved, the glaring ſun declines.

THE brighteſt wit in the world, without the better qualities of the heart, muſt meet with this fate; and tends only to endear ſuch a character as I take yours to be. In the better diſcovery, and fuller conviction of which, I have a ſtrong opinion, I ſhall grow more and more happy, the longer I live your acquaintance, and (if you will indulge me in ſo much pleaſure)

Your faithful friend, and moſt

obliged ſervant,

A. POPE.

LET-

꙳꙳꙳꙳꙳꙳꙳꙳꙳꙳꙳꙳꙳꙳꙳꙳꙳꙳꙳꙳꙳꙳꙳꙳

LETTER II.

MADAM,

Twitenham, Nov. 5.

THOUGH I am · extremely obliged by your agreeable letter, I will avoid all mention of the pleafure you give me, that we may have no more words about compliments; which I have often obferved people talk themfelves into, while

they

they endeavour to talk themfelves out
of.   It is no more the diet of friendfhip and efteem, than a few thin wa-
fers and marmalade were of fo hearty
a ftomach as Sancho's.   In a word,
I am very proud of my new relation,
and like Parnaffus much the better,
fince I found I had fo good a neigh-
bour there.   Mrs. H——, who lives
at court, fhall teach two country-folks
fincerity; and when I am fo happy
as to meet you, fhe fhall fettle the
proportions of that regard, or good-
nature, which fhe can allow you to
fpare me, from a heart, which is fo
much her own as yours is.

THAT

THAT lady is the moſt truſty of friends, if the imitation of Shakeſpear be yours; for ſhe made me give my opinion of it with aſſurance it was none of Mrs ——. I honeſtly liked and praiſed it, whoſe-foever it was; there is in it a ſenſible melancholy, and too true a picture of human life; ſo true an one, that I can ſcarce wiſh the verſes yours at the expence of your thinking that way, ſo early. I rather wiſh you may love the town (which the author of thoſe lines cannot *immoderately* do) theſe many years.

It

It is time enough to like, or affect to like, the country, when one is out of love with all but one's-felf, and therefore ftudies to become agreeable or eafy to one's-felf. Retiring into one's-felf is generally the *pis-aller* of mankind. Would you have me defcribe my folitude and grotto to you? what if, after a long and painted defcription of them in verfe (which the writer I have juft been fpeaking of could better make, if I can guefs by that line,

No noife but water, ever friend to thought)

I   what

what if it ended thus?

What are the falling rills, the pendant fhades,
The morning bow'rs, the evening colonnades;
But foft recesses for th' uneafy mind,
To figh un-heard in, to the passing wind!
Lo! the ftruck deer, in fome fequefter'd part,
Lies down to die (the arrow in his heart);
There hid in fhades, and wafting day by day,
Inly he bleeds, and pants his foul away.

If thefe lines want poetry, they do
not want fenfe. God Almighty long
preferve you from a feeling of them!
The book you mention, Bruyere's
Characters, will make any one know
the world; and I believe at the fame

C   time

time defpife it (which is a fign it will make one know it thoroughly). It is certainly the proof of a mafter-hand, that can give fuch ftriking likeneffes, in fuch flight fketches, and in fo few ftrokes on each fubject. In anfwer to your queftion about Shakefpear, the book is about a quarter printed, and the number of emendations very great. I have never indulged my own con-jectures, but kept meerly to fuch amendments as are authorized by old editions, in the author's life-time: but I think it will be a year at leaft before the whole work can be finifh-ed.

ed. In reply to your very handfome (I wifh it were a very true) compliment upon this head, I only defire you to obferve, by what natural, gentle degrees I have funk to the humble thing I now am: firft from a pretending poet to a critick, then to a low tranflator, laftly to a meer publifher. I am apprehenfive I fhall be nothing that's of any value, long, except,

  Madam,

   Your moft obliged, and

    moft faithful humble

    fervant,

     A. POPE.

I long for your return to town;
a place I am unfit for, but fhall
not be long out of, as foon as I
know I may be permitted to
wait on you there.

LET-

※※※※※※※※※※※※※※※※※※※※※※※※※※

LETTER III.

MADAM,

Thurſday night.

IT was an agreeable ſurprize to me, to hear of your ſettlement in town. I lye at my Lord Peterborow's in Bolton-ſtreet, where any commands of yours will reach me to-morrow, only on Saturday-evening I am pre-engaged. If Mrs. H—— be to be en-

gaged

gaged (and if fhe is by any creature,
it is by you), I hope fhe will join us.
I am, with great truth,

Madam,

Your moft faithful friend,

and obliged fervant,

A. POPE.

LET-

LETTER IV.

MADAM,

I COULD not play the imperti-
nent so far as to write to you,
till I was encouraged to it by a piece
of news Mrs H —— tells me, which
ought to be the most agreeable in the
world to any author, That you are
determined to write no more — It is
now the time then, not for me only,

but

but for every body, to write without fear, or wit: and I fhall give you the firft example here. But for this affu-rance, it would be every way too dangerous to correfpond with a lady, whofe very firft fight and very firft writings had fuch an effect, upon a man ufed to what they call fine fights, and what they call fine writings. Yet he has been dull enough to fleep quietly, after all he has feen, and all he has read; till yours broke in upon his ftupidity and indolence, and totally deftroyed it. But, God be thanked, you will write no more; fo I am in

no danger of increaſing my admira-
tion of you one way; and as to the
other, you will never (I have too
much reaſon to fear) open theſe eyes
again with one glimpſe of you.

I AM told, you named lately in a
letter a place called Twitenham, with
particular diſtinction.   That you may
not be miſ-conſtrued and have your
meaning miſtaken for the future, I
muſt acquaint you, Madam, that the
name of the place where Mrs. H——
is, is not Twitenham, but Richmond; which your ignorance in the
geography

geography of thefe parts has made
you confound together. You will
unthinkingly do honour to a paltry
hermitage (while you fpeak of Twitenham) where lives a creature altogether unworthy your memory or
notice, becaufe he really wifhes he
had never beheld you, nor yours.
You have fpoiled him for a folitaire,
and a book, all the days of his life;
and put him into fuch a condition,
that he thinks of nothing, and en-
quires of nothing but after a perfon
who has nothing to fay to him, and
has left him for ever without hope of

ever

ever again regarding, or pleafing, or entertaining him, much lefs of feeing him. He has been fo mad with the idea of her, as to fteal her picture, and paffes whole days in fitting before it, talking to himfelf, and (as fome people imagine) making verfes; but it is no fuch matter, for as long as he can get any of hers, he can never turn his head to his own, it is fo much better entertained.

D 2   LET-

✻✻✻✻✻✻✻✻✻✻✻✻✻✻✻✻✻✻

LETTER V.

MADAM,

I AM touched with fhame when I
look on the date of your letter.
I have anfwered it a hundred times
in my own mind, which I affure you
has few thoughts, either fo frequent
or fo lively, as thofe relating to you.
I am fenfibly obliged by you, in the
comfort you endeavour to give me

upon

upon the lofs of a friend. It is like the fhower we have had this morning, that juft makes the drooping trees hold up their heads, but they remain checked and withered at the root: the benediction is but a fhort relief, though it comes from Heaven itfelf. The lofs of a friend is the lofs of life; after that is gone from us, it is all but a gentler decay, and wafting and lingering a little longer. I was the other day forming a wifh for a lady's happinefs, upon her birth-day: and thinking of the greateft climax of felicity I could raife, ftep by ftep, to

I   end

end in this — a Friend. I fancy I have fucceeded in the gradation, and fend you the whole copy to afk your opinion, or (which is much the better reafon) to defire you to alter it to your own wifh: for I believe you are a woman that can wifh for yourfelf more reafonably, than I can for you. Mrs. H ——— made me promife her a copy; and to the end fhe may value it, I beg it may be tranfcribed, and fent her by you.

To

To a Lady, on her Birth-day,

1723.

Oh! be thou bleſt with all that heaven can ſend:
Long life, long youth, long pleaſure—and a friend!
Not with thoſe toys the woman-world admire,
Riches that vex, and vanities that tire:
Let joy, or eaſe; let affluence, or content;
And the gay conſcience of a life well-ſpent,
Calm every thought; inſpirit every grace;
Glow in thy heart; and ſmile upon thy face!
Let day improve on day, and year on year;
Without a pain, a trouble, or a fear!
And ah! (ſince death muſt that dear frame deſtroy),
Dye by ſome ſudden extacy of joy:
In ſome ſoft dream may thy mild ſoul remove,
And be thy lateſt gaſp, a ſigh of love!

PRAY,

P R A Y, Madam, let me fee this mended in your copy to Mrs. H——; and let it be an exact fcheme of happinefs drawn, and I hope enjoyed, by yourfelf. To whom I affure you I wifh it all, as much as you wifh it her.

I am always, with true refpect,

Madam,

Your moft faithful friend,

and moft humble fervant,

A. P O P E.

L E T-

LETTER VI.

MADAM,

Twitenham, Aug. 29.

YOUR laſt letter tells me, that if I do not write in leſs than a month, you will fancy the length of yours frighted me. A conſciouſneſs that I had upon me of omitting too long to anſwer it, made me look (not without ſome fear and trembling) for

E   the

the date of it: but there happened to
be none; and I hope, either that you
have forgot how long it is, or at leaft
that you cannot think it fo long as I
do, fince I writ to you. Indeed a
multitude of things (which fingly
feem trifles, and yet altogether make
a vaft deal of bufinefs, and wholly take
up that time which we ought to value
above all fuch things) have from day
to day made me wanting, as well to
my own greateft pleafure in this, as
to my own greateft concerns in other
points. If I feem to neglect any
friend I have, I do more than feem to

neglect

neglect myfelf, as I find daily by the increafing ill conftitution of my body and mind. I ftill refolve this courfe fhall not, nay I fee it cannot, be long; and I determine to retreat within myfelf to the only bufinefs I was born for, and which I am only good for (if I am entitled to ufe that phrafe for any thing). It is great folly to facrifice one's felf, one's time, one's quiet (the very life of life itfelf), to forms, complaifances, and amufements, which do not inwardly pleafe me, and only pleafe a fort of people who regard me no farther than a

E 2   meer

meer inftrument of their prefent idle-
nefs, or vanity. To fay truth, the
lives of thofe we call great and happy
are divided between thofe two ftates;
and in each of them, we poetical fid-
lers make but part of their pleafure,
or of their equipage. And the mi-
fery is, we, in our turns, are fo vain
(at leaft I have been fo) as to chufe
to pipe without being paid, and fo
filly to be pleafed with piping to
thofe who underftand mufick lefs than
ourfelves. They have put me of late
upon a tafk before I was aware, which
I am *fick* and *fore* of : and yet enga-
ged

ged in honour to fome perfons whom
I muft neither difobey nor difappoint
(I mean two or three in the world
only) to go on with it. They make
me do as mean a thing as the greateft
man of them could do; feem to de-
pend, and to folicit, when I do not
want; and make a kind-of court to
thofe above my rank, juft as they do
to thofe above theirs, when we might
much more wifely and agreeably live
of ourfelves, and to ourfelves. You
will eafily find I am talking of my
tranflating the Odyffey by fubfcrip-
tion: which looks, it muft needs
look,

look, to all the world as a defign of mine both upon fame and money, when in truth I believe I fhall get neither; for one I go about without any ftomach, and the other I fhall not go about at all.

THIS freedom of opening my mind upon my own fituation will be a proof of truft, and of an opinion your goodnefs of nature has made me entertain, that you never profefs any degree of good-will without being pretty warm in it. So I tell you my grievances; I hope in God you have none,

none, wherewith to make me any return of this kind. I hope that was the only one which you communicated in your laft, about Mrs. H—— filence; for which fhe wanted not reproaches from me; and has fince, fhe fays, amply atoned for. I faw a few lines of yours to her, which are more obliging to me than I could have imagined: if you put *my welfare* into the fmall number of things which you heartily wifh (for a fenfible perfon, of either fex, will never wifh for many), I ought to be a happier man than I ever yet deferved to be.

UPON

UPON a review of your papers, I have repented of fome of the trivial alterations I had thought of, which were very few. I would rather keep them till I have the fatisfaction to meet you in the winter, which I muft beg earneftly to do; for hitherto methinks you are to me like a fpirit of another world, a being I admire, but have no commerce with: I cannot tell but I am writing to a Fairy, who has left me fome favours, which I fecretly enjoy, and fhall think it unlucky,

unlucky, if not fatal, to part with. So pray do not expect your verfes till farther acquaintance.

F LET-

LETTER VII.

MADAM,

Twitenham, Sept. 30, 1722.

NO confidence is fo great, as that one receives from perfons one knows *may be* believed, and in things one is *willing* to believe. I have (at laft) acquired this; by Mrs. H——— repeated affurances of a thing I am

unfeign-

unfeignedly fo defirous of, as your allowing me to correfpond with you. In good earneft, there is fometimes in men as well as in women, a great deal of unaffected modefty: and I was fincere all along, when I told her perfonally, and told you by my filence, that I feared only to feem imperti-nent, while perhaps I feemed negli-gent, to you. To tell Mrs. —— any thing like what I really thought of her, would have looked fo like the common traffick of compliment, that pays only to receive; and to have told it her in diftant or bafhful terms,

would

would have appeared fo like coldnefs
in my fenfe of good qualities (which
I cannot find out in any one, without
feeling, from my nature, at the fame
time a great warmth for them) that I
was quite at a lofs what to write, or
in what ftile, to you. But I am re-
folved, plainly to get over all objec-
tions, and faithfully' to affure you, if
you will help a bafhful man to be paft
all preliminaries, and forms, I am
ready to treat with you for your
friendfhip. I know (without more
ado) you have a valuable foul; and
wit, fenfe, and worth enough, to make

me

me reckon it (provided you will permit it) one of the happineffes of my life to have been made acquainted with you.

I DO not know, on the other hand, what you can think of me; but this, for a beginning, I will venture to engage, that whoever takes me for a poet, or a wit (as they call it), takes me for a creature of lefs value than I am: and that where-ever I profefs it, you fhall find me a much better man, that is, a much better friend, or at leaft a much lefs faulty one, than I

am

am a poet. That whatever zeal I
may have, or whatever regard I may
fhew, for things I truly am fo pleafed
with as your entertaining writings;
yet I fhall ftill have more for your
perfon, and for your health, and for
your happinefs. I would, with as
much readinefs, play the apothecary
or the nurfe, to mend your head-akes,
as I would play the critick to improve
your verfes. I have ferioufly looked
over and over thofe you intrufted me
with; and affure you, Madam, I
would as foon cheat in any other
truft, as in this. I fincerely tell you,

I can

I can mend them very little, and only in trifles, not worth writing about; but will tell you every tittle when I have the happinefs to fee you.

I AM more concerned than you can reafonably believe, for the ill ftate of health you are at prefent under: but I will appeal to time, to fhew you how fincerely I am (if I live long enough to prove myfelf what I truly am)

  Madam,

   Your moft faithful fervant,

    A. POPE.

     I am

I am very fick all the while I write
this letter, which I hope will
be an excufe for its being fo
fcribbled.

×××××××××××××××××××××××××××××

L E T T E R VIII,

MADAM,

Twitenham, Nov. 9.

IT happened that when I determined to anſwer yours, by the
poſt that followed my receipt of it,
I was prevented from the firſt proof
I have had the happineſs to give you
of my warmth and readineſs, in re-

G   turning

turning the epitaph, with my sincere
condolements with you on that melancholy subject. But nevertheless I
resolved to send you the one, though
unattended by the other: I begged
Mrs. H—— to inclose it, that you
might at least see I had not the
power to delay a moment the do-
ing what you bid me; especial-
ly when the occasion of obeying
your commands was such, as must
affect every admirer and well-wish-
er of honour and virtue in the nation.

. You

You had it in the very blots, the better to compare the places; and I can only say it was done to the best of my judgement, and to the extent of my sincerity.

I DO not wonder that you decline the poetical amusement I proposed to you, at this time. I know (from what little I know of your heart) enough at least to convince me, it must be too deeply concerned at the loss, not only of so great, and so near a relation; but of a good man (a loss

G 2   this

this age can hardly ever afford to bear, and not often can fuftain). Yet perhaps it is one of the beft things that can be faid of poetry, that it helps us to pafs over the toils and troubles of this tirefome journey, our life; as horfes are encouraged and fpirited up, the better to bear their labour, by the jingling of bells about their heads. Indeed, as to myfelf, I have been ufed to this odd cordial, fo long, that it has no effect upon me: but you, Madam, are in your honey-moon of poetry; you have feen only the fmiles, and enjoyed the careffes,

of

of Apollo. Nothing is fo pleafant to a Mufe as the firft children of the imagination; but when once fhe comes to find it meer conjugal duty, and the care of her numerous progeny daily grows upon her, it is all a four tax for paft pleafure. As the Pfalmift fays on another occafion, the age of a Mufe is fcarce above five and twenty: all the reft is labour and forrow. I find by experience that his own fiddle is no great pleafure. to a common fidler, after once the firft good conceit of himfelf is loft.

I LONG

I LONG at laſt to be acquainted
with you; and Mrs. H —— tells me
you ſhall ſoon be in town, and I bleſt
with the viſion I have ſo long deſired.
Pray believe I worſhip you as much,
and ſend my addreſſes to you as often,
as to any female Saint in Heaven: it
is certain I ſee you as little, unleſs it
be in my ſleep; and that way too,
holy hermits are viſited by the Saints
themſelves.

I AM, without figures and meta-
phors, yours: and hope you will
think,

think, I have fpent all my fiction in my poetry; fo that I have nothing but plain truth left for my profe; with which I am ever,

Madam,

Your faithful

humble fervant.

LETTER IX.

MADAM,

Five o'clock.

I THINK it a full proof of that unlucky ftar, which upon too many occafions I have experienced; that this firft, this only day that I fhould

2   have

have owned happy beyond expec-
tation (for I did not till yefterday
hope to have feen you fo foon) I
muft be forced not to do it. I
am too fick (indeed very ill) to go
out fo far, and lie on a bed at my
doctor's houfe, as a kind of force
upon him to get me better with all
hafte.

I AM fcarce able to fee thefe few
lines I write; to wifh you health and
pleafure enough not to mifs me to-
day, and myfelf patience to bear

H being

being abfent from you as well as I can
being ill.

I am truly,

Your faithful fervant,

A. P O P E.

LETTER X.

MADAM,

Jan. 17, 172²⁄₄.

AFTER a very long expecta-
tion and daily hopes of the fatisfaction of feeing and converfing
with you, I am ftill deprived of it in
a manner that is the moft afflicting,
becaufe it is occafioned by your ill-

H 2   nefs

nefs and your misfortune. I can
bear my own, I affure you, much
better: and thus to find you loft to
me, at the time that I hoped to have
regained you, doubles the concern I
fhould naturally feel in being deprived of any pleafure whatever.

MRS. H—— can beft exprefs to
you the concern of a friend, who
efteems and pities: for fhe has the
liberty to exprefs it in her actions, and
the fatisfaction of attending on you
in your indifpofition.

I WISH

I WISH sincerely your condition were not such as to debar me from telling you in person how truly I am yours. I wish I could do you any little offices of friendship, or give you any amusements, or help you to what people in your present state most want, better spirits. If reading to you, or writing to you, could contribute to entertain your hours, or to raise you to a livelier relish of life, how well should I think my time employed! indeed I should, and think it a much better end of my poor studies, than

all

all the vanities of fame, or views of a character that way, which engage moſt men of my fraternity.

IF you thoroughly knew the zeal with which I am your ſervant, you would take ſome notice of the advice I would give you, and ſuffer it to have a weight with you proportionable to the ſincerity with which it is given.

I BEG you to do your utmoſt to call to you all the ſuccours, which

I   your

your own good fenfe and natural re-
flexion can fuggeft, to avoid a melancholy way of thinking, and to throw
up your fpirits by intervals of mode-
rate company; not to let your diftem-
per fix itfelf upon your mind at leaft,
though it will not entirely quit your
body. Do not indulge too much
folitarinefs. Though moft company
be not proper or fupportable during
your illnefs, force yourfelf to enter
into fuch as is good and reafonable,
where you may have your liberty,
and be under no reftraint.

WHY

WHY will you not come to your
friend Mrs. H——, fince you are
able to go out, and fince motion ·is
certainly good for your health ? why
will you not make any little fets of
fuch as you are eafieft with, to fit
with you fometimes ?

Do not think I have any interefted
aim in this advice : though I long to
fee you, and to try to amufe you, I
would not for the world be confi-
dered as one that would ever require

for

for my own gratification, any thing that might either be improper or hurtful to you.

PRAY let me know, by our friend Mrs. H——, if there can be any thing in my power to ferve, or to amufe you. But ufe me fo kindly, as not to think ever of writing to me till you are fo well as that I may fee you, and then it will be need-lefs. Do not even read this, if it be the leaft trouble to your eyes or head.

I   BELIEVE

BELIEVE me, with great refpect, and the warmeft good wifhes for your fpeedy recovery,

Madam,

Your moft faithful,

and moft humble fervant,

A. P O P E.

※※※※※※※※※※※※※※※※※

LETTER XI.

MADAM,

Twitenham, June 2, 1723.

IT was an inexpreffible pleafure to
me to fee your letter, as I affure
you it had long been a great trouble,
to reflect on the melancholy reafon
of your filence and abfence. It was

I 2 that

that only which hindered my writing, not only again, but often, to
you; for fear your good-nature
fhould have been prompted to oblige
me too much at your own expence,
by anfwering. Indeed I never ex-
preffed (and never fhall be able to
exprefs) more concern and good wifhes for you, than I fhall ever feel for
one of your merit.

I A M forry, the moment you grow
better, to have you fnatcht from
thofe, who I may fay deferve the pleafure of feeing you in health, for

having

having fo long lamented and felt your illnefs.

Mrs. H——, I hope, will find it not impoffible to draw you to Richmond: and if not, I dare fay will not be long out of Hertfordfhire. I want nothing but the fame happy pretence fhe has, of a title through your friendfhip, and the privilege of her fex, to be there immediately. I cannot but wonder you have not heard from her, though I fhould wonder if any body elfe had; for I am told by her family fhe has had

much

much of the head-ake at Bath, befides the excufe of a great giddinefs
occafioned naturally by the waters.
I writ to her at the firft going, and
have not had a word from her; and
now you tell me the fame thing, I
conclude fhe has been worfe than I
imagined. I hear fhe returns on
Wednefday, when I fhall have the fatisfaction (I doubt not) to talk and
hear a great deal of Mrs. ———.

I WISH I could fay any thing, either to comfort you when ill, or entertain

tertain you when well. Though nothing could, in the proper proportion of friendſhip, more affect me than your condition; I have not wanted other occaſions of great melancholy, of which the leaſt is the loſs of part of my fortune by a late act of parliament.

I AM at preſent in the afflicting circumſtance of taking my laſt leave of one of the * trueſt friends I ever had, and one of the greateſt men in all polite learning, as well as the moſt

* Biſhop Atterbury.

agreeable

agreeable companion, this nation ever had.

I REALLY do not love life fo dear-ly, or fo weakly, as to value it on any other fcore, than for that portion of happinefs which a friend only can be-ftow upon it: or, if I muft want that myfelf, for the pleafure which is next it, of feeing deferving and virtuous people happy. So that indeed I want comfort; and the greateft I can re-ceive from you (at leaft unlefs I were fo happy as to deferve what I never can) will be to hear you grow better

I   till

till you grow perfectly well, perfectly
eafy, and perfectly happy, which no
one more fincerely wifhes than,

    Madam,

        Your faithful and obliged

           friend and fervant,

             A. POPE.

K   LET-

✳✵✺✵✺✵✺✵✺✵✺✵✺✵✺✵✺✵✺✵✺✵✺✳

L E T T E R XII.

MADAM,

Twitenham, Sept. 26, 1723.

IT would be a vanity in me to tell
you why I trouble you so soon
again: I cannot imagine myself of
the number of those correspondents
whom you call favourite ones; yet I
know

know it is thought, that induſtry may make a man what merit cannot : and if an old maxim of my Lord Oxford's be true, That in England if a man reſolve to be any thing, and conſtantly ſtick to it, he may (even a Lord Treaſurer): if ſo, I ſay, it ſhall not be want of reſolution that ſhall hinder me from being a favourite. In good earneſt, I am more ambitious of being ſo to you, Madam, than I ever was, or ever ſhall be, of being one to any Prince, or (which is more) any Prince's Miniſter, in Chriſtendom.

I WISH

I wish I could tell you any agreeable news of what your heart is concerned in; but I have a fort of quar-
rel to Mrs. H—— for not loving
herfelf fo well as fhe does her friends;
for thofe fhe makes happy, but not
herfelf.

There is an air of fadnefs
about her which grieves me, and
which, I have learnt by experience,
will increafe upon an indolent (I will
not fay an affected) refignation to it.

It

It will do fo in men, and much more
in women, who have a natural foft-
nefs that finks them even when reafon does not. This I tell you in confidence; and pray give our friend
fuch hints as may put her out of hu-
mour with melancholy; your cen-
fure, or even your raillery, may
have more weight with her than
mine: a man cannot either fo de-
cently, or fo delicately, take upon
him to be a phyfician in thefe con-
cealed diftempers.

You

You see, Madam, I proceed in
trusting you with things that nearly
concern me. In my last letter I spoke
but of a trifle, myself: in this I ad-
vance farther, and speak of what
touches me more, a friend.

This beautiful season will raise up
so many rural images and descriptions
in a poetical mind, that I expect, you,
and all such as you (if there be any
such), at least all who are not down-
right dull translators, like your ser-

I   vant,

vant, muft neceffarily be productive
of verfes.

I LATELY faw a fketch this way
on the bower of * BEDINGTON: I
could

---

* The lines here alluded to are as follows:

In Tempe's fhades the living lyre was ftrung,
And the firft Pope (immortal Phœbus) fung,
Thefe happy fhades, where equal beauty reigns,
Bold rifing hills, flant vales, and far-ftretch'd plains,
The grateful verdure of the waving woods,
The foothing murmur of the falling floods,
A nobler boaft, a higher glory yield,
Than that which Phœbus ftampt on Tempe's field:

All

could wifh you tried fomething in the
defcriptive way on any fubject you
pleafe, mixed with vifion and moral;
like pieces of the old provençal poets,
which abound with fancy, and are
the moft amufing fcenes in nature.
There are three or four of this kind
in Chaucer admirable: " the Flower
and the Leaf" every body has been
delighted with.

All that can charm the eye, or pleafe the ear,

Says, Harmony itfelf inhabits here.

I HAVE

I HAVE long had an inclination to tell a Fairy tale, the more wild and exotic the better; therefore a *vision*, which is confined to no rules of pro-bability, will take in all the variety and luxuriancy of defcription you will; provided there be an apparent moral to it. I think, one or two of the Perfian tales would give one hints for fuch an invention: and perhaps if the fcenes were taken from real places that are known, in order to compliment particular gardens and buildings of a fine tafte (as I believe

L   feveral

several of Chaucer's descriptions do, though it is what nobody has observed), it would add great beauty to the whole.

I wish you found such an amusement pleasing to you: if you did but, at leisure, form descriptions from objects in nature itself, which struck you most livelily, I would undertake to find a tale that should bring them all together: which you will think an odd undertaking, but in a piece of this fanciful and imaginary nature I

I   am

am fure is practicable. Excufe this
long letter; and think no man is more

Your faithful

and obliged fervant,

A. POPE.

CONTENTS.

LET-

THE END.